Lost and Found

by Marie Langley • illustrated by Cheryl Cook

Summer vacation was great, but now time was beginning to drag, and it was just getting to the stage where the question "What shall we do today?" was becoming harder to answer.

Carlos, Cindy, and Talia were sitting on the front porch of Talia's house, considering their options while they waited for Kane to show up. He usually had the best ideas, even if sometimes they were a little crazy—like his idea that they build a pedal-powered flying machine in the backyard. Yet even that gave them something to argue and laugh about.

Conversation had crawled to a standstill, and silence was settling in on the sunny porch.

That didn't last long, though. The sound of running footsteps announced the arrival of Kane. He came charging around the corner of the house, waving a piece of yellow paper, and threw himself onto the porch alongside his friends.

"Look!" announced Kane, gasping to get his breath back. "We have to do this!"

"We have to do what?" asked Cindy.

"It's a scavenger hunt." Kane handed the piece of paper to Cindy, and Talia and Carlos crowded around her to look at it, too.

"You get two hours to find a whole list of things in the neighborhood, and bonus points if you do it in less time. It'll be really fun! We have to do it!" Kane was obviously eager, but no one replied—they were too busy reading the flier, and besides, they knew from experience not to agree to any of Kane's ideas too quickly.

"It's being run by the recreation center as part of their summer program," said Talia. "It's a good prize, bowling tickets, and it's a team thing too." Carlos was beginning to warm to the idea.

"But look at the rules," said Cindy. "There has to be an adult with each team. And look at this rule—each team can only have three members."

"Oh, no!" Talia sat back, looking grumpy, and added gloomily that she was just starting to like the idea. Besides, how would they find an adult to help them on a weekday?

"And," Cindy reminded them, "there are four of us, and it won't be fair if one of us can't be on the team."

Kane reached over to take the flier. "When is it again?" he asked as he quickly scanned the text. "It's not until Friday, so that gives us time to come up with a plan."

"Hang on, I might be able to solve one problem right now." Talia jumped up and went into the house. The others stayed on the porch looking at the flier again and wondering what items would be on the list.

Soon Talia came back outside, followed by her dad. Talia beamed as she explained that her dad worked from home and that he could make time to help them.

Talia's dad, Mr. Hart, smiled at everyone. "It'll be great to tag along. It sounds like fun," he said.

Everyone began chattering excitedly about the scavenger hunt, but Carlos seemed distracted.

"Hey, guys." From the tone of his voice, it sounded as if Carlos had something important to say. "About the team number problem—I've got an idea."

It took some discussion before Carlos convinced his friends that his idea was a good one. At first, they had trouble accepting that the group of friends would be separated during the contest, but they had to agree that Carlos had come up with a good solution.

Carlos planned to convince his younger brother and one of his cousins to join him and form another scavenger hunt team. And he was sure his aunt would be the adult for this second team. She was always telling the kids to get up off the couch and be more active, so Carlos said she'd be happy for them to participate. She didn't work on Fridays either, so that shouldn't be a problem.

"So," said Carlos, "even if we can't be on the same team, we'll still all get to take part in the scavenger hunt."

"And now we know what we're doing today," said Kane, jumping up. "We're signing up at the rec center. Let's go!"

It was Friday morning, and the scavenger hunt was about to begin. Cindy, Kane, Talia, and Mr. Hart all wore large stickers that read "Scavenger Hunt, Team 10." They stood by a bulletin board outside the recreation center, reading the rules for the event.

"It says each of the 20 teams will be given a different list. Some of the items will be the same, and some will be different," said Cindy, "and no buying or stealing any items."

An announcement came over the sound system that had been set up outside the center. "Adult members from all teams, please assemble at the registration desk to collect the envelope containing the list of items for your team. Do not open your envelope until you're instructed to do so."

The crowd moved and shuffled as the adults made their way to the registration desk. Talia spotted Carlos and his family, but there was only time for a quick wave to Carlos before Mr. Hart returned and the next announcement came over the speaker.

"Final reminders, people. Team members must remain together at all times. There are points awarded for each item you find. Final report-back time is 12 noon, but if you finish earlier, you may receive bonus points. The team with the most points wins the scavenger hunt. A full copy of the rules appears on the back of your list. You may now open your envelopes—the hunt is on!"

Mr. Hart tore open the envelope with a flourish, took out a sheet of paper, and passed it to Talia. "Over to you three now," he said. Mr. Hart reminded them that he wasn't allowed to help with the hunt; his job was just to see that they all stayed safe.

Talia, Cindy, and Kane carefully studied the items on the list, and Cindy suggested that they start with something they were sure they could find.

"Good call," said Kane enthusiastically, "but we'll also need to make a plan so we don't waste time running around in circles."

"We can start with this one," said Talia, pointing to the third item on the list that read: one oak leaf. "There's a big oak tree in the square by the library."

There was a flurry of movement; the teams began rushing off in various directions as if a huge gust of wind were blowing them all away. Team 10 ran toward the library while Carlos urged Team 15 to follow him in the opposite direction.

Scavenger Hunt List

1. confetti
2. water bottle
3. one oak leaf
4. footprint
5. used bus ticket
6. feather
7. brochure
8. receipt
9. coffee cup
10. rubber band
11. chopsticks
12. dandelion

Five minutes later, Team 10 reached the town square, where Talia ran to the enormous old oak tree and grabbed a leaf from the ground beneath. "That was easy," she said. "What's next?"

Kane studied the list. "We should be able to find a feather here before we move on," he said, "because there are plenty of pigeons around, and we only need a single loose feather!"

But it wasn't that easy—the birds seemed to be holding on to their feathers tightly. Mr. Hart sat on a bench by the library, watching with amusement as the three friends ran around the square, sending pigeons fluttering in all directions.

"We're wasting time here!" complained Cindy. "Fifteen minutes have passed, and we've only found one item."

"I think we should move on. There'll be birds in other places too, and if not, we can come back here and try again later, if we have time," Talia suggested.

"We might find a few things on the list over near the mall." As soon as Kane announced this, the friends were off, running down the sidewalk with Mr. Hart hurrying to keep up.

As they passed a bus shelter near the entrance to the mall, Cindy swerved inside and grabbed something that was lying on the ground, just as it was about to be snatched up by a boy wearing a Team 17 sticker. "Cross the used bus ticket off the list," called Cindy.

Kane said he guessed it must be on Team 17's list too, and he wondered what everyone else was looking for. The other scavenger hunt teams they could see were all scurrying around and searching for items.

"We can't worry about them," Talia told him. "Let's just focus on our own list. So what else do we need?"

Kane showed her the list. There were still ten items left.

Kane collected an empty water bottle from a woman who was about to put it in a trash can. She looked surprised when Kane asked if he could have it, but smiled when she saw his sticker.

As items were being checked off, time was also ticking by, and Cindy was getting anxious. "There are two weird things still on the list," she said. "Confetti and a footprint. We're going to run out of time!"

"Let's go to the party store inside the mall," said Talia. "There's sure to be confetti there. Maybe customers will have spilled some when they filled their bags, but the footprint ... How on earth will we accomplish that?"

"And don't forget the feather!" Kane reminded them.

Sure enough, Team 10 found a small scattering of confetti near the fill-it-yourself bins. Cindy and Talia quickly collected some confetti from the floor after they checked with the store clerk that it would be okay. Outside the store, Kane picked up a larger piece of paper from the ground. It was a sales flier, but Kane wasn't reading the ad—he was staring at the back of it.

"This is fantastic!" he exclaimed. "Look what I found!" On the back of the paper was a clear print of someone's foot. To anyone else, the paper with its dirty print was just a piece of trash, but to Team 10, it was one more important item that they could now cross off their list.

"Oh, wow! Now there's only the feather left to collect!" Cindy was a lot happier. "We can do this!"

"Maybe," said Talia. "What's the time, Dad?"

Mr. Hart checked his watch and told them it was nearly noon. He added that they'd better hurry because they only had ten minutes to get back to the rec center.

"That's not enough time to retrace our steps *and* get back to the library," cried Cindy, "so let's just hope we find a feather on the way to the finish line. Come on!"

There were no feathers on the way back to the recreation center. "Never mind," said Talia. "We'll check in with what we've got."

Carlos was in the crowd near the check-in desk, and they were pleased to see him. "Hi, Carlos! How'd it go? Where's the rest of your team?"

Carlos shrugged. "We hardly found anything on our list, and even though the kids had fun, they got too tired, so my aunt took them home. I was waiting here to see how you guys did."

"We found everything except a feather," said Cindy.

"Really? A feather was on our list too, and we actually found two." He pulled a feather from his pocket. "Do you want it?"

Cindy reached out and briefly touched the feather, but then she stopped and turned back to her team, and they had a rapid, whispered conversation.

"Thanks a lot, Carlos," said Talia, "but we don't think it would be fair when we didn't find the feather ourselves. Will you wait for us while we check in?" Carlos nodded.

As Team 10 walked to the desk, Mr. Hart spoke quietly. "Well done, team," he said. Mr. Hart added that he was very proud of them for making that last decision, and that whatever happened, they were a great team.

"Thanks, Dad," said Talia, and the others smiled.

A woman at the desk was calling them. "Welcome back, Team 10! Time's almost up, so you're our last team."

"No bonus points for us, then," said Cindy. "And anyway," she added gloomily, "we're one item short, so I guess we've blown any chance of winning."

"Doesn't matter," Talia chimed in. "It was still fun."

Team 10 carefully spread all of their items out on the desk, and the woman checked each item off the list before asking them to go and wait with everyone else.

They returned to Carlos and excitedly told him about everything that had happened during the hunt. They were laughing about Kane's having asked the woman for her empty water bottle when the sound system boomed to life.

"Okay, folks," said the announcer. "I'm sure you're anxious to hear the results, and we'll get to that very soon."

"Come on," Cindy muttered. "Let's get this over with so we can go home and relax."

"Shhh!" said Talia. Cindy rolled her eyes.

The announcer continued, "First, I'd like to thank all of the competitors for taking part, and special thanks to the adults who found time to be with their teams. I also want to thank all those who spent so much time organizing this event. And now I'm sure you want to know which team won. It was very close!"

There was a rustling of paper over the sound system as the announcer paused to decipher the results that had been written down.

"Two teams came out ahead of all the other teams. Team 17 finished first, which means they collected the most time-bonus points." There was a small burst of cheering.

"However, Team 17 only managed to bring back eight of their twelve items," the announcer continued, "while the other team found the most items from their list, with a total of eleven out of the twelve."

"Hey! That's us!" said Kane. The crowd was applauding once more.

"That team also happened to be the last to finish, right at the final moment, so no bonus points there, but their high score for the number of items was enough to put them one point ahead of Team 17. So, congratulations to the winners of this year's scavenger hunt—Team 10!"

There was loud clapping and cheering from the crowd and surprised laughter from Cindy, Kane, and Talia. Carlos was as pleased as they were.

"You need to go get your prize," Mr. Hart told them, so all three went forward and were given their bowling tickets.

"We can't go bowling without Carlos," said Cindy thoughtfully as they tried to navigate their way back through the crowd. The others agreed, and by the time they reached Carlos and Mr. Hart, they had found a solution.

The four friends decided to share the cost of the fourth ticket for Carlos. They offered to do the same for Mr. Hart, but he insisted that if he came with them, he would buy his own ticket, especially since they wouldn't let him pay for the one for Carlos.

"So that's decided," said Kane, grinning. "Now, when shall we go bowling?!"

Summarize

Use the most important details from *Lost and Found* to summarize how the four friends rethought ideas during their adventure. Your graphic organizer may help.

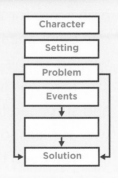

Text Evidence

1. How can you tell this story is realistic fiction? Identify two features that tell you this. GENRE

2. There are several problems that cause the friends to rethink their ideas. List some of the problems and explain how each one was solved or avoided. PROBLEM AND SOLUTION

3. Using the surrounding text, figure out what the idiom "tag along" means on page 4. IDIOMS

4. Write about a problem Carlos had with his team and how it affected his plan to take part in the scavenger hunt. WRITE ABOUT READING

Compare Texts
Read about friends who try out different ideas to
complete a challenge.

It's a Challenge

It was the first week of summer vacation, and Annie was
hosting a slumber party. All day, she'd been bursting with
excitement, and now her four friends had finally arrived.

"What shall we do first?" asked Hayley, and the girls
thought about their options.

Then Mr. Kerrisk, Annie's dad, suggested a party game,
telling them it was a team challenge.

"What do we have to do?" asked Annie.

"You have to pass a balloon from person to person across
the room without dropping or bursting it."

"That sounds easy," scoffed Katrina, but it wasn't quite that
easy—they couldn't touch the balloon with their hands or feet.

"We could do it like this," said Annie, trying to tuck the balloon under her chin—but the balloon was too big.

Katrina suggested that they use their teeth, but when she tried, the balloon make a squeaking noise like it was about to pop. She laughed and said, "Maybe not."

Straws wouldn't work either because the girls couldn't get enough suction to hold on to the balloon.

"I know!" said Sami. "We can bounce it on our heads!"

The girls kept the balloon bouncing from head to head, and although a couple of times it almost escaped, they finally managed to reach the far end of the room.

They all agreed that the game had been fun.

"Well done, team!" said Mr. Kerrisk. "You met the challenge, so now you deserve some refreshment." He opened the door through to the dining room to reveal a table set up with delicious snacks, and over in the corner were five large, colorful balloons.

"Fantastic!" exclaimed Annie. "We can think of more balloon challenges while we eat!"

Make Connections

How do the friends in *It's a Challenge* figure out the best way to move the balloon? ESSENTIAL QUESTION

How do the rules of a game make the friends in *Lost and Found* and *It's a Challenge* rethink their ideas? TEXT TO TEXT

Focus on Literary Elements

Dialogue Writers of fiction use dialogue to tell us exactly what characters say. They put quotation marks around the words that a character says, and use verbs such as *said*, along with the character's name, to let us know who spoke the words. Writers have some other ways to show us who is speaking, as well as how they sound.

Read and Find

- The writer uses *said* and the character's name:
  "Good call," said Kane ... (page 7)

- The context of the spoken words indicates who is speaking:
  "We might find a few things on the list over near the mall."
  As soon as Kane announced this ... (page 8)

- A different verb tells you how the character spoke:
  "We're wasting time here!" complained Cindy. (page 8)

Your Turn

Copy the chart below. Find two examples in *Lost and Found* to match each of the types of dialogue listed on the left, and write all the examples you find on the chart.

Dialogue	Examples
Using *said*	
Using the sentence context	
Using a verb other than *said*